Darling Acres

The Breakdown Poems

Amy M. Vaughn

Corpse Flower Press

Corpse Flower Press

Tucson, Arizona

Copyright © 2021 Amy M. Vaughn

ISBN: 978-0-578-31065-7

DEDICATION

For Rich

1

Every day I walk around my neighborhood
The same path
every morning
and
every night

My neighborhood is called
Darling Acres
I shit you not

2

I walk every day because I am
recuperating
from scarred veins and
busted valves
in my leg
because I lost the Covid vaccine lottery
Blood clots
1 in 100,000 chance
C'est la vie
So it goes

It's a nice enough neighborhood
Darling Acres
Small mid-century homes
skinny sidewalks
dogs on leashes
people with small bags of poop who say
"morning"
The people say morning, the poop bags don't
That would be weird
Darling Acres is not weird

3

Sometimes when I walk I am lost in thought
and I have to remind myself to look at the sky
BE HERE NOW and all of that
The sky here is so blue it's stunning
After a rain settles the dust
the blueness of the sky could kill a person
It's that intense
Happens all the time

4

Walking early you see the go-getters
Spandex
Lycra
Racing bikes
Later on it's old people and parents with strollers
At night it's no one
or homeless people
or drunk ones and twos walking home from the bar
She's carrying her shoes in one hand
He's laser-beaming the asphalt with his eyes
visualizing and executing
every step

5

One spring
I was working in the front yard
keeping Darling Acres darling
when an old woman crossed the street
coming right for me
No one else around

"I don't know where I am," she said
"Where are you coming from?"
"I don't know."

Before long I had fetched her a folding chair
and a plastic tumbler of ice water
She told me she had a daughter
but she couldn't remember her name
and she had three grandkids
whose names she could remember just fine
She relaxed a bit
talking about them
while my mind spun with
"What the fuck am I gonna do with this lady?"

I called 911
What is the opposite of a missing person?
After a long afternoon, it turned out she had
deliberately left
not wandered away
from a care home just around the corner
A house I walk by every day

"I don't live there," she said. "That is not my home"

After that, new squares of paper were hung
in the bedroom windows
of the house where she was kept
the paper facing in
I wondered what they said
THIS IS YOUR HOME NOW

Today, walking by that house
a young woman in scrubs sat on the low retaining wall
near the putrid garbage cans
in a deep and skunky waft of weed

6

I have to go off lithium
to fix the swelling
and pain
in my leg
So this little adventure just got a fuck of a lot more interesting

7

For more than three months
For a season
A fiscal quarter
I've woken up to pain
and spent my days walking
resting, elevating, icing, soaking
managing the ache, the burn, the stabbing, shocking, sandpaper sensations
Tomorrow I can take pain meds
Real ones, not shitty acetaminophen that does nothing

Tomorrow

8

To distract myself
when it is too hot to walk
I watch season after season
of a Japanese game show
where comedians try to make each other laugh
Every season it devolves into literal dick jokes
Ball touching
Hard ons
Hiding things in foreskins
Convalescing with only network TV must have sucked

9

When I'm unmedicated
my bipolar
manic depression
mood swings
happen every month
like clockwork
like a period

One day I wake up with
extra low self-worth
anhedonia
irrational paranoia
and if it's really bad
suicidal ideation

A week to ten days later
I wake up with
rapid thoughts, pressured speech
zero impulse control
creative obsession
delusions of grandeur
and if it's really bad
suicidal ideation

But there's always Xanax
Better a pharmaceutical straight jacket for one day
than a trip to the psych ward for three

10

Sleep is the best
only
escape
Xanax makes the sleep come
Otherwise the second I close my eyes
my being lights up with the limb on fire
Xanax, yes sir

11

In Darling Acres
we have no HOA
so you can have a junked-up car in your yard
for as long as you want
or paint your house purple
But it's written into the title that no one can live in your garage
or in any outbuilding

Darling Acres fears the Fonz

12

The greater saphenous vein is the longest vein in the human
body

13

4 Stars—worth the struggle

The full-leg compression sock sleeve tube device
takes preparation and patience
to put on
But it helps
up to a point
about 8 hours later

8 hours of feeling
a quarter mummified
a quarter peg legged
a quarter itching in direct sunlight

When the leg has HAD ENOUGH
and there is no patience left
to get it off
It has to be NOW

Within the hour the pain is roaring
and I wonder why I ever took off
the full-leg compression sock sleeve tube device

14

Soon, as in within days
when the insurance company gives me its blessing
I'll make an appointment to have
the greater saphenous vein
in my left leg
ablated
cauterized
burned shut

The thought of it gives me the squirms
but within weeks
I should be able to
stand in one place again
sit with my feet on the floor
have less (no?) pain
sleep without drugs
do shit around the house
do shit outside of the house
besides walk around
Darling Acres

15

Hello
Is it bedtime?
Can I take Xanax now?

16

Telehealth

for psychiatry

and the incoming call is late

How long do I wait to call them?

How long before I seem needy, anxious, neurotic?

How long before it will be written in my city-phone-book-sized chart?

Go in my Brandon-Sanderson-fantasy-novel-brick-thick folder?

*

I called

after 7 minutes

"Your appointment was moved. You should have received an email"

An email?

Who does that kind of thing by email?

"But while I have you one the phone, do you want to take care of your co-pay?"

17

Darling Acres used to be a farm
with an orchard of orange trees
Darling was the farmer's last name
In his honor, or perhaps at his request
every house had orange trees planted out front
two each
lining the street
Several of these orange trees are still around
60-plus years later
Nice-sized leafy green trees that blossom in the spring
and smell like perfume wishes it could smell
They put out fruit that is big and bright and hard and sour
Homeless people, hungry people, pluck them from the trees
take one bite and drop them to the ground
Oranges ripen and fall into the road to be run over
And for the rest of the summer
the sidewalks and streets of Darling Acres
are strewn with rotting fruit

18

Today is a make-it-through-the-day day
A cup-o-noodle, diet coke, brainless television day
I'm tired and sore and grumpy
This compression sleeve on my leg is itchy
and slides down if I twitch
WHAT ARE YOU GRATEFUL FOR?
Fuck off, please
But listing what you're grateful for makes you feel better
(butterfly, flower, heart emoji)
Today I am grateful I don't have to pretend to be grateful

19

In a blink
everything I've ever done
is rendered ridiculous
every compliment I've received
has been a lie

I'm a joke
I'm a fool
I'm less than nothing, a waste of space
annoying
deluded
unwanted

At least some day I will die

Then I smile
chat
and make dinner

20

I thought I wanted to teach college
so I did
I taught philosophy
back when I was
unmedicated
undiagnosed
unmisdiagnosed even

I hated teaching
I hated grading
I hated every new batch of hateful eyes
Or maybe I was having bipolar episodes all the fucking time
and blaming my job
instead of my brain
Maybe
So I quit
Since then I have had six different job titles
and 16 different jobs

Now my job is to walk around Darling Acres
to lessen the chance of another clot in my leg
or an embolism in my lungs
or an aneurism in my brain

It's a living

21

Last night I didn't walk around Darling Acres
because friends came over
stayed late
I was tired

In bed, nearly asleep
I felt a tightness in my calf
the same as when the first clots came

I jumped out of bed and walked
my heart going fast
walked walked walked

The next day
I still have fear

22

It is one of the wettest years on record
and everything's growing like crazy
The weeds are wild in people's rock yards and driveways
Mesquite limbs hang low

An urban legend going around says the ground is so saturated
the shallow-rooted saguaro
that grow only here
are toppling over
but I haven't seen that in Darling Acres

Gnats and mosquitoes are everywhere
and these tiny black beetles
that were getting into the bathroom by the dozens
until we noticed the window crank could turn a little more

There's water in the fireplace

The Texas sage has blossomed twice and
the road oranges are moldy

Silt, sand, pebbles, rocks
washed down the streets
form deltas
in the crossroads

I have always been a fan of
rain in the desert

Open the doors

Go out and stand
palms face up

But everything this rain brings now
means work
on the yard, on the roof
Work I can't do
Work and narrowing sidewalks
in Darling Acres

23

Sylvia Plath
Ann Sexton
Diane motherfucking di Prima
These are the poets who raised me

I read their terse, honed words
about men
about children
about kitchens

And like any angst-filled teenage
idealist
I thought, not me

Then I got
a man
a child
a kitchen

Sylvia Plath
Ann Sexton
Diane motherfucking di Prima
I'm listening

24

Having my feet in the air
holds an entirely different kind
of pleasure
for me these days

25

Sometimes when I'm walking my loop of
Darling Acres
I imagine what it was like when the desert shrubs and cactus
were small
when the houses were new and
pristine
and husbands would all pull out of the driveway at exactly
8 AM
in gas-guzzling steel behemoths
like in Edward Scissorhands
And wives would corral the children
off to school
go back inside to their vacuum and their valium
watch As the World Turns
gossip on short-corded telephones
and wait for Betty Friedan to tell them
the gaping void they felt
was not a defect
or their fault

26

Anhedonia
the absence of pleasure
is a good word to know
when you have depression
or know someone who does
and that covers pretty much all of us

It's the feeling of not feeling
Not sad, not angry, not irritated
no matter how your slack face
might appear to others

You can look right at things that would normally
set you off or
get you going
and . . . nothing

Basic questions
What do you want for dinner?
Want to watch a movie?
Answers come slowly if at all

Nothing calls to you
You fall back on habit
or say, "You choose. I don't care"
and mean it, deeply

It's easy to see how nothing matters
how choices are hollow

how tiny our lives are
blips on the timeline

But though this is depression
this is not despair
This is anhedonia

27

Sometimes
rarely
but sometimes
I get tired of saying thank you

28

Depression makes my eyes heavy
Lets me sleep when I'm not tired
Takes my words away

I hide it from most everyone
but especially my son
Pull up the mouth corners
Show some teeth

But my heavy eyes
give me away

29

Just resting up to take a shower

30

Today on my morning walk I saw the old
light blue Ford
out for a tentative test drive
and a good-sized watermelon
just one
growing in the yard of someone
who has home health care workers
visit every day

Then the surgery scheduler called and said
insurance denied the blood tube cauterization
to fix my leg

They're going to keep working on it
she assured me

31

I write because I have nothing better to do
I write because I can't hold a job
I write because I can't go anywhere
I write because I have no talent
for painting
or clay
or people

But I am not a writer
I don't want to be
and it's one of those things you have a choice in
calling yourself a writer

I tried it, didn't like it
I wrote six books
or seven

It would be fine
great even
if being a writer only meant writing
but it doesn't

It also means
submitting
networking
constantly marketing your self
All acts my fragile psyche can't abide
So I might write
but I will not be a writer

32

Hey, can I tell you something
as if we were friends
because we are, right,
we're friends?
Yeah, we're friends

The thing is, my husband
he likes it better when I'm depressed
No, not like that
He doesn't *like it* when I'm depressed
he would just rather I be depressed
than manic
if given a choice

How cruel! To wish that on someone
Being manic can
at least for a minute
here and there
be a blast!

His point is
when I'm depressed
I *think* about killing myself
When I'm manic
I accidentally might

33

Nothing like chronic pain
for paring life back and finding out
what's most important to you
and that Circle K Coke Icees are on the top of that list

34

I am not old
If I were old
the next two weeks
the time between now and
when my surgeon defends the
medical necessity
of burning up this busted vein
to the insurance rep
would fly by
To hear them tell it
old people
blink and a day's gone by
No, I am not yet old

35

The treadmill was going too fast
"Blow on my wrist"
said the woman in the lab coat with the clip board
(the lab coat didn't have the clip board, the woman did
otherwise that would be weird
but this dream wasn't in Darling Acres
so weirdness was allowed)
I held her wrist to my mouth
and tried to remember to breathe
while my legs flailed
always on the edge of succumbing

36

It rained last night
again
and was supposed to be raining this morning
but wasn't
which meant I could walk outside
instead of in one place while reading a book
which isn't all bad
But it's September now
and the rains will end soon
if tradition and not new
scary patterns dictate

There were puddles and
the tiny leaves of desert trees each held
that one light-refracting drop
that didn't fall
but would transfer to a hand, a head
if touched

Overcast skies
still rare enough to remind me
of the luxury to be out walking beneath them
and not behind a desk
in front of a class
behind a register
A luxury gained by trading away
stability
independence
self-worth

but thinking like that will make you
crazy
Better to enjoy the wet morning after
what could be
the last rain of the season

37

Hold on
Just let me catch my breath
before I cut that cantaloupe

38

When my heart spills over
for the guy waving a flag
in front of the secondhand store
for the woman with too many bags
at the bus stop
for the meth head filling his backpack with ice
at the Circle K
I know I'm teetering on manic

When I believe I am not moral enough
giving enough
good enough
as long as I have what others do not
a washer and dryer
a shower
more than two pairs of shoes
When I find myself on the brink of giving it all away
When I catch myself before I act
I still feel guilty for having what others do not
but so far, I've managed to keep my life
intact

39

I have a routine from which
I dare not deviate
or BAD THINGS will happen

I have bracketed free time
in which to express free will
just like everybody else

But I have to be careful not to let spontaneity
creep in
not to get
obsessed
It could mean getting off schedule
It could mean extra pain
It could mean an explosion or a full stop

After half a lifetime of finding joy
accomplishment
and meaning
in spontaneous manic obsession
a schedule is a strait jacket

When I eat is dictated by when I take drugs
When I rest by when I walk
by the expectations of pets
by other people's day jobs
and class times

It's not so different really
from real life
from working and parenting
except the pain
and constant threat of
explosion or full stop

It's the absence of freedom of movement that
whittles away at choice
until the days that used to
fly by
grow long
blur together
and disappear

40

Read trash
Watch trash
Scroll trash
So much time
to do something
productive
Like read the dead white classics
Like take up (another) cause
Like make real connections
with strangers
who may
or may not
be who they say they are

41

I'm sorry kiddo
that you won't be able to live
where you grew up
that the desert was never meant
to host this many people

I'm sorry about Phoenix

Water will be too expensive
People will leave
No tax-base, no infrastructure
No consumers, no jobs

But if you move north
with the climate
you're bound to find someplace
you feel at home

42

Alexa, how many people have bipolar?
2.8% of the U.S. population has some form of bipolar disorder
That's around 6,000,000 people

Just kidding
I don't have an Alexa device

43

If I back off the pain meds enough
to not bleed from my kidneys
it doesn't so much take my pain away
as make wearing the
unsexiest thigh highs
more tolerable
which is a win
I guess

44

Maybe being off lithium
my memory will come back
I won't struggle to find words
I won't call the can opener
the sharp circle metal cutter

There's a word for words escaping you
but it escapes me right now
I shit you not

Maybe being off lithium
nothing will change
and I'll discover it wasn't the drug
it was me
all along

Pull a craptastic reverse Dumbo

45

Downward comparison is a drug
I know people have it worse than me
hurt more than me
more permanently (hopefully?) than me

I know compared to them I am a tourist

I wonder if they have meetings where they compete
speaking in their code
"I've been at a 7+ all week"
"I haven't been able to shower since June"

And when Rachel sobs in the corner
they shake their heads
"Novice"

I don't belong at those meetings
I'm not on their level

But downward comparison can get you in trouble
can make you think, this isn't so bad
I can tough it out
instead of accepting this situation for what it is
apart from theirs
instead of remembering how it felt to be you
instead of fighting
for what you need

46

I added a cul-de-sac to my walk around Darling Acres
out of disdain for the fat in my earlobes

The houses there are bigger
with better rooves and
art piece mailboxes

There were butterflies and wild bunnies

But the sidewalks are full of gravel and grass
because no one has time to deal with the
unexpected messes left behind by the rain

And this stately sleepiness is still surrounded
on all four sides
by flowing multilane traffic
by engine noise
car horns
sirens

Just like the rest of us

47

There is a code you can decipher
if you've had
or been close to
chronic pain

If you ask, "How are you?"
And they say, "Hanging in there."
If you ask, "How have you been?"
And they say, "Some days are better than others."

That's code for
"Today is a shit day and
you're kind of a shit for asking."

48

The more I live isolated in the middle of this city
the less it means to me
and
the more I want to move
somewhere isolated

where I can walk on green paths
and never encounter a soul
where I can see for miles
during the day
and all the stars at night

49

My eyes are tired

Phone
Laptop
Phone
Kindle
TV
Laptop
Phone
TV
Phone
Kindle

No wonder

50

Before we moved to Darling Acres
we rented a small(er) house
closer to the center of the city
on the historic registry
with a plaque out front and everything

It had cut glass doorknobs
and two square feet of kitchen counterspace
We were robbed twice
once for each year we lived there

The first time we went to the grocery store we saw
two women holding hands
"Look! Lesbians!" I whispered
because before we moved
behind the hipster cult video store and bar
in a neighborhood with homelessness and urban farming
we lived in a typical, small Arizona town
Fox news on at the tire store
the doctor's office
the hairdresser's

Lesbians in public was huge for me
Their freedom meant my freedom
And yes, I guess it is better to be trapped in Darling Acres
than still in my hometown

51

Every morning I hear weed whackers
but when I walk
I can never tell whose house
the noise
was coming from

52

Tugging on a new compression leg sleeve
Replace every 4 to 6 months
$50 a pop
Holy shit how do old women do this?
I failed to notice it pushing the blood
up my leg
into my torso
out my other leg
and arms
bloop bloop bloop
until I was filled up, laid out
like a 98° waterbed
and the cat crawled on to take a nap

53

Reading
Sam Pink
Justin Grimbol
John Konrath
Big Bruiser Dope Boy

Where are the women
underground poets
confessors
not writing about love
or if they do
doing it right

Give it to me straight
in as few words as possible
Save your florid bullshit for
greeting cards

54

True crime TV
is the freak show of our day
for people who think they live safe lives
to gawk at
feel that frisson
that chill
"That could have been me"

True crime TV
is exploitation
we can all agree on

55

I wrote a "poem"
and now I'm trying to pretend
that's enough
to make today worth it
to be worth today

Now I've written two

56

Young me
sitting cross legged on a concrete bench on campus
rapt by the motion of ants beneath me

How could anyone ever be bored
when there is so much intricacy, mystery around us
so much marvel?

Who needs more than eyes?

Manic? yes
but I still wonder how people
can live without wonder

57

I am "a failed suicide attempt is just a cry for help" years old
emphasis on *failed* and *just*

I think about killing myself
or being dead
a few times a day
when I'm not busy

I was 14 the first time I thought
Maybe I could just die
Scared the crap out of me
30+ years later
I'm used to it

Pain, age, fatness, regular wear and tear
I could just die
Humans are disposable
We have a shelf life

It's all very factual
Not morbid
Not sad
The thought comes
regardless of mood
I could die
One of not many solutions

I don't want to die
my brain just reminds me

that it's an option
It's the stairwell door next to the elevator
You could always take the stairs
but you never do

If I'm busy
obsessed with a project
there is no room for the death thought
But manic obsession wrecks my life
and I've gotten pretty good
at nipping it in the bud

In trade, the thought comes
I could just die
But as long as I don't dwell
as long as I don't start making plans
it passes quickly

And I always know that someday I *will* die
and no longer have to put up with these thoughts
about dying all the time

58

Another day
Another loop
or three
around Darling Acres

Chit-chatting with elderly neighbors
Scoping license plates of work-at-homes
who moved here
when Covid took over
from Idaho
California
Colorado
for their reasons

Nodding hello to the landscapers
out in force
with their wide brimmed hats
and long-sleeved white shirts
with their black metal trailers
and bucket-lifts for useless palm trees
with more work than they've had in living memory
because of the rains

It's going to be over 100 degrees
every day this week
September in the desert
So we're all out early
in Darling Acres
getting shit done

before the sun
tries to kill us
Get in line sun
Get in line

59

I need a retreat
a sabbatical
from pain and limits and dependency
on others
Two weeks
Two months
A season
Then I can come back fresh
ready to face my constraints
with renewed enthusiasm
or at least
half a shred of dignity

60

When Covid was new and all
nonessential
businesses were closed or
went to work-at-home
Darling Acres was crawling
with walkers, bikers, families
pulling their smallest in a wagon

It was a block party
every evening at dusk
where people waved and yelled hello
from the other side of the street

The guy next door
put tape on the road
at even intervals
and worked on his wheelies

But then it got hot
No one walks in the summer here
except those of us who are
recuperating
from injury
fatness
age
depression

It picked back up in the fall
but wasn't the same
and didn't last
The novelty was gone
just like it was for home improvements
and baking bread

61

Remember
after 9/11
everyone was nice to each other
for a week or two?
Unless your skin was brown
or you wore a turban
Maybe,
if the grays crash land a ship
a fleet of ships
into the coast of California
clear some beach front real estate
take out sacred Hollywood
we could be civil to each other
for a whole month

62

The body tightens
around pain
to protect itself
and tension spreads
Aches, knots, fatigue
miles away from the origin

Relax relax relax
But stop paying attention and
it's back
the defense causing offense
the pain causing pain

63

Surrounding myself
with wants
with wishes
with whens
Pulling them into the hole
burying them in the yard
for later

64

Patience runs thin
when it's been
ridden rough
and the end is in sight

even if it's a mirage

65

Feeling the unsupervised freedom
of a kid left at home
when her parents go out
because
the old ladies
best friends
who live in the houses
I can see from my window
are both away on vacation

66

A middle-aged woman
in a flyover state
who writes without grace
about everyday things

who believes with de Beauvoir
that the only meaning in life
is the meaning we give it

who believes in the
intrinsic value of every life
which makes us all equal
and means starting from scratch
everyone just as
important and meaningless
as everyone else

who every few weeks is
certain
of the choices she's made
about where to attribute meaning

in people and animals
and words

but being authentic
(and what's more important than that?)
Sartre says
means never forgetting that

all meaning
where you attach
what you love
is a construct
that comes from within
and is hardly more than
a coping device
(or, if you ask science, an evolutionary trick)
to keep us from running away
when love feels abstract

The only question
said Camus
is suicide
is whether or not to kill yourself

This is why I don't
but could be why I do

67

I walk at 8, noon, 4, and at night
after the temperature drops
below 90 degrees
so I
we
can walk outside

I walk at night
with my husband
my partner of
twenty years
Twenty Years

And the first thing we do
is find the moon
and if it looks especially cool
has clouds around
is big or orange or both
we plan our walk to maximize the view

While we walk he tells me
about his day
and what he has coming up
We talk about domestic shit
that has to be sorted out
And I point to especially overgrown yards
and say *They have a lot of work to do*

Night walks
under the moon
and the five stars we can make out beyond
the city haze
(one of them probably Venus)
with Darling Acres
quiet
watching wide screen TVs
they wish were wider
or maybe already in bed
or possibly having kinky sex
in the guest bedroom/dungeon
but I doubt it
are my favorite part of the day
unless someone brings me a Coke Icee
Then they are my second

68

Soon I'll find out
when the procedure
surgery
cauterization
will be
Insurance or no

On my walk I thought
I should use the time between now and the
big day
as a retreat
from social media
from terrible television shows
from angst and worry and fear

But pain makes it hard to center
without distraction it
looms large in consciousness
And trying to willfully quell that
sets me up for failure
so
you know
fuck that

Instead I'll try to remember to
relax relax relax
when I feel my brow furrow
my shoulders swallow my neck
I'll try to remember to enjoy

no
appreciate
no
be present for
these (hopefully) last few days
weeks
before the pain intensifies
before healing begins again
before life takes its finger
off the pause button

69

Night pain
in the quiet
is the worst

No

Awaking to pain
is the worst
because it makes you
sad, angry, disappointed
to be conscious
Fuck
not this again

70

In and out
of talk therapy
for decades
and never has a counselor
a therapist
an assessor
a psychologist
a psychiatrist
asked me about my dreams

One grizzled old hippie
with toenail claws
curling over his Birkenstocks
told me "dreams are the day's
mind garbage
There's rarely deeper meaning
Now listen to this singing bowl"

71

Surgery is scheduled
35 days from today

72

I somehow got five slivers
walking through Darling Acres

A six-foot wall of pigweed
blocks an alley
utility trucks could drive through
at the start of summer

The shaded Texas sage
is in its third bloom

When I was a
for real activist
the first
climate change projection map
I saw
said this desert would become
much wetter
but since then they've all said
drier and hotter

Maybe in 2031 everyone in Darling Acres
will be growing watermelons
in their front yards

73

I missed the window
to walk outside
before the sun was fully armed
and spraying death rays

but getting back to sleep
after night pain
for the first time
in four months
was worth it

and reading on the treadmill has its charm

74

A month
A whole month
Just one more month
One more are-you-fucking-kidding-me month

And that's just until they
dope me up
and run a cable up my vein to
burn the fucker shut

Then 5 days
of bandages
Then stitches out
Then back in the compression sleeve

A week when it'll be
"pretty bad, especially at night"
Then 1 or 2 weeks more
Then then then
That should do it

6 months from day 1

75

My son's girlfriend was here again last night
She accepted a cookie from my hand
Soon we will make eye contact
I'm sure of it

76

I am learning
again
that it's okay
to let things slide

77

My dentist
who is a very quiet man
who speaks slowly with
long pauses
with whom I am patient
because
statistically speaking
he's likely depressed
and could suicide any minute
asked
"Any medication changes?"
"I'm off lithium"

For the first time in seven years
his face changed
He looked me in the eye
"That's great," he said
"That's really great"

I didn't explain

78

Writer?
No thanks, I'm trying to quit
I'm a much better reader
cheerleader
organizer
but I can't seem to stop
putting words on paper
Call it what you will

79

I wore a hole in my walking shoes
and have to break in a new pair
They were waiting in my closet
and I immediately ordered another set
to take their place
This is who I am now

80

My big dream
is to live very small
with quiet days
close friends
and complete acceptance

81

I am prone to agoraphobia
A year and a half at home
due to Covid and
Covid-related clots
means I have an
unimaginable amount of
very uncomfortable work
ahead of me

82

There are worse places to live
worse times to be alive
worse people to be surrounded by
worse afflictions to suffer from

Downward comparison
to the rescue

83

At 10 am I was fine
At noon I felt a little off
By 2 pm depression had
rolled in and
taken over

Brought to you by rapid cycling bipolar

84

My path around Darling Acres
is disappearing
Grass tendrils reach
combine and weave
through tan dirt and gray pebbles
obscuring the sidewalk
Bushes grow tall and form
a canopy
Tree limbs droop and must
be ducked or pushed away
Spiders are common and
the lizards have grown large
Until the next yard
clean bright sunny and boring

85

Sometimes all I can think is
I need help
I need help getting places and
doing things
sure
But that's not really what I mean
I mean
I need help staying on the planet
and what good is that?
Somebody who needs help just
to be
on a planet that's bursting its seams
What good is that?
Taking up space
and resources
to struggle just
to be

You have to help yourself says
my upbringing
the economy
the hustle and grinders

Help yourself by helping others says
my upbringing
the feminine
the do-gooders

But needing help just to stay
on the planet?
Nobody talks about that
And if nobody talks about it
does it exist?
Should it?

86

"We're put on this earth to help each other"
That's a pretty dumb system
if we're all reaching over our own needs
for others
Like that game of stacked hands
where the bottom one comes on top
over and over and over
faster and faster and faster
until it all falls apart
and it's just empty space
where the hands were

87

Sorry
We will only be serving
gallows humor
for the time being

88

I don't understand
how people don't think
about killing themselves
every day

89

Spent the second half of this morning's walk wiping away tears and

breathing through my lips
because
I spent the first half of this morning's walk wondering if
my reasons to live
were really worth it

Right around the halfway point
it dawned on me
that this is what lithium fixed
that I used to be used to this
that this is dangerous

I came home and emailed
(who does this sort of thing through email?)
my psychiatrist
Short-term counseling?
Get back on lithium and
forego the pain meds
until closer to the
vein ablation?

So now I'm waiting for his reply
and trying not to think about
how much I've been thinking about
killing myself

90

Daytime Xanax is such a drag
when I'm not manic
but that's the plan
until the lithium levels
are back
where they need to be

91

Back at it
walking like a zombie
through Darling Acres
because the leg does not care about
breakdowns
or lithium head
or the pain medication that is
rapidly exiting my body

The leg just is
just like Darling Acres
and the world around it

Don't expect too much

92

Lithium doesn't give me a high
Lithium doesn't *give* anything
It only takes
It takes my memories and words
along with the death thoughts
and obsessions
the paranoia and delusions

You lose some
you lose some

93

People have asked
If you knew this would happen
knew you'd get blood clots and
go through all this
would you have gotten the vaccine?

If I knew it would play out
exactly as it has
and be over after six months
I would have
because life is long and
it looks like
Covid isn't going anywhere

I have enough to fear

But will I be getting a booster?
Oh, fuck no

94

Bipolar means always having to say you're sorry

95

Darling Acres
sounds like a funny farm
doesn't it?

Welcome to Darling Acres
What insurance do you have?

Great. Now take this pill
and this one
Oh, and it looks like
doc says
this one too

If you can still walk
you're welcome to enjoy
the manicured grounds
or watch TV in the dayroom

Group sessions are cancelled
because of Covid
and therapy will be over the phone

But we'll keep you safe
until the drugs stabilize
and then we'll let you go
pretending you're healed

Won't that be nice?

96

Hiding behind the blinds
waiting for the loud lady
with the two yipping dogs
to clear my street
before I venture out
into Darling Acres

97

If I can
hang tough
for a couple more days
things will get better

I've taken lithium
on and off
but mostly on
for the last few years
but I've never front loaded
it like this
always built up gradually

My thoughts move like mosquitos
in jagged stuttering paths
then disappear
when I reach out for them

When I focus
all that's there
is the ringing in my ears

I wanted to say something
meaningful
about the pandemic
taking away community
forcing life smaller
inside walls
about the pain in my leg

taking away mobility
forcing life smaller
inside mind
about lithium
taking away my thoughts
forcing life smaller
to each moment
What is now?
Have I eaten?
Am I clean?

Long blank stare
and then
I have a pen in my hand
I must be writing

But I haven't thought about
killing myself today
because "killing myself" is part of
anything
and I can't think about
anything
at all

98

I have met Maslow's hierarchy
I am fed
sheltered
loved
accomplished
creative

I've overcome past trauma and
had peak experiences

I've raised a healthy, happy child
and helped people
in significant ways

And yet
it's hard to feel like a successful
or even normal
adult
when you have the emotional lability
of a teenager

But bipolar isn't my fault
any more than having brown eyes
or this bum leg

It's part of who I am
It's shaped my perception
increased my empathy
and I wouldn't trade it for anything

Just kidding
Fuck that
I would shed it in an instant
for some other life
if it meant
less fear
less pain
less guilt
less grief

99

I have been culturally
conditioned to think
I need to end this collection
with roses
and hope

Things went wrong
but I fixed them
and so can you!
(sunshine, smiley face, heart emoji)

But I haven't fixed anything
I've just wrapped the glitchy part
of my brain
in Saran Wrap
and slid it to the back of the fridge

100

Surgery is scheduled
20 days from today

ABOUT THE AUTHOR

Amy M. Vaughn is the author of several weird little books, including *The Shelter*, *Freak Night at the Slee-Z Motel*, and *Skull Nuggets*. She edited the bizarro writing prompt collection *Dog Doors to Outer Space* and has short stories in several anthologies. *Darling Acres* is her first poetry collection.

Amy lives in Tucson, Arizona in a small house with her small family. You can find her online on social media or at amymvaughn.com.

STATE
OF
MIND

A STORY OF MENTAL HEALTH

KESHAN SINGH

Tellwell Talent
www.tellwell.ca

ISBN
978-0-2288-7574-1 (Paperback)
978-0-2288-7575-8 (eBook)